THE CHICKEN COOKBOOK

TIGER BOOKS INTERNATIONAL
LONDON

Introduction

The growth in popularity of chicken has been impressive. At one time most people ate whole roast chicken once a week with the usual potatoes, gravy and two vegetables. Not any more. The much publicized nutritional value of chicken has now meant that eating chicken three times a week is not unusual.

Unlike red meat, chicken is low in fat, but is still high in protein and rich in important vitamins. As well as being healthy, chicken is also a very versatile meat. It is quick and easy to cook, and its flavour combines well with almost every herb, spice and vegetable imaginable. Chicken also has the added advantage of tasting great whether it is served hot in a curry, or cold in a salad. Chicken is therefore a great ingredient for the summer months when it can be used very successfully in picnics, buffets, barbecues and salads.

Another reason for the growth in popularity of chicken is the huge range of ways it can now be bought. At one time you could buy a whole chicken, fresh or frozen, and that was that. Today you can buy drumsticks, breasts, thighs, and quarters, or a mixture of these, as well as free-range chicken, corn-fed chicken and poussins. The smaller family and single people can now enjoy chicken, too, as it comes in small packs containing enough to serve just one or two.

As well as old favourites, you will find many delicious food ideas from around the world in this book, as well as a few old favourites. Each recipe is in an easy-to-follow format and has a full-colour photograph of the end result to help you achieve good results. So, whether it is an impressive dinner or a quick mid-week meal, choose chicken and you can be sure of success.

3289
This edition published in 1993 by Tiger Books International PLC, London
© 1993 Coombe Books
Printed and bound in Singapore
ISBN 1 85501 309 6

Tamarind Chicken Satay

Traditionally satay is served only as part of a meal,
but this version is so good that is needs only a tomato
sambal as an accompaniment.

SERVES 4

4 chicken breasts, skinned, boned and cut
    into 1.25cm/½-inch cubes

Marinade
1 tbsp oil
5 cm/2-inch piece tamarind, soaked in
    120ml/4 fl oz hot water or lemon juice
2 cloves garlic, crushed
1 tsp ground cardamom
½ tsp ground nutmeg
Salt and pepper
1 tsp sweet soy sauce

Tomato and Chilli Sambal
2 red chilli peppers
1 small piece fresh ginger, grated
1 clove garlic, crushed
450g/1lb fresh tomatoes, peeled and
    seeded
60ml/4 tbsps oil
1 tbsp lemon or lime juice
1 tbsp dark brown sugar
Salt and pepper

1. Put the chicken in a large bowl. Mix
together the marinade ingredients and
pour them over the chicken. Stir well and
refrigerate for at least 30 minutes.

2. Grind together the chillies, ginger and
garlic in a food processor or a pestle and
mortar. Chop the tomatoes coarsely and
blend them into the chilli mixture.

3. Heat the oil in a wok or large frying
pan and fry the tomato mixture for about
5-6 minutes, stirring occasionally to
prevent it sticking. Add the lemon juice
and a spoonful of water, if the sauce
becomes too thick.

4. Stir in the sugar and seasoning to taste.
Set aside.

5. Thread the marinated chicken cubes
onto thin wooden skewers.

6. Cook the chicken under a preheated
grill, turning frequently, until golden
brown – about 5-8 minutes. Brush the
chicken with the remaining marinade
during cooking. Serve the satay with the
tomato and chilli sambal.

TIME: Preparation takes about 30 minutes, and cooking takes 10-15 minutes.

PREPARATION: The chicken satay can be cooked very successfully on
an outdoor barbecue grill.

Terrine of Spinach and Chicken

*This superb terrine is ideal when you want to
impress your guests with a delicious appetizer.*

SERVES 6-8

225g/8oz chicken breast meat, skinned
2 egg whites
120g/4oz fresh white breadcrumbs
450g/1lb fresh spinach, washed
1 tbsp each of fresh finely chopped
    chervil, chives and tarragon
Freshly ground black pepper
280ml/½ pint double cream
60g/2oz finely chopped walnuts
Pinch nutmeg

---

1. Cut the chicken into small pieces.

2. Put the cut chicken, 1 egg white and half of the breadcrumbs into a food processor. Blend until well mixed.

3. Put the spinach into a large saucepan and cover with a tight-fitting lid.

4. Cook the spinach for 3 minutes, or until it has just wilted.

5. Remove the chicken mixture from the food processor and rinse the bowl.

6. Put the spinach into the food processor along with the herbs, the remaining egg white and breadcrumbs. Blend until smooth.

7. Season the chicken mixture with a little pepper and add half of the cream. Mix well to blend thoroughly.

8. Add the remaining cream to the spinach along with the walnuts and the nutmeg. Beat this mixture well to blend thoroughly.

9. Line a 450g/1lb loaf tin with greaseproof paper. Lightly oil this with a little vegetable oil.

10. Pour the chicken mixture into the base of the tin and spread evenly.

11. Carefully pour the spinach mixture over the chicken mixture, and smooth the top with a palette knife.

12. Cover the tin with lightly oiled aluminium foil and seal this tighly around the edges.

13. Stand the tin in a roasting dish and pour enough warm water into the dish to come halfway up the sides of the tin.

14. Cook the terrine in a preheated oven 160°C/325°F/Gas mark 4 for 1 hour, or until it is firm.

15. Put the terrine into the refrigerator and chill for at least 12 hours.

16. Carefully lift the terrine out of the tin and peel off the paper. To serve, cut the terrine into thin slices with a sharp knife.

TIME: Preparation takes 25 minutes, cooking takes 1 hour.

SERVING IDEA: Serve slices of the terrine on individual serving plates
garnished with a little salad.

CHICKEN LIVER PÂTÉ

*Deceptively quick and easy to prepare, this
creamy pâté is sure to be a firm favourite.*

SERVES 4

30g/1oz butter, for frying
1 clove garlic, crushed
1 onion, finely chopped
Salt and pepper
225g/8oz chicken livers, trimmed
1 tsp Worcestershire sauce
60g/2oz butter, creamed
1 tbsp brandy

1. Heat the butter in a frying pan and add the garlic, onion, and salt and pepper. Fry gently, until the onions have softened, but not coloured.

2. Increase the heat and stir in the chicken livers. Sauté for about 2 minutes on each side, stirring continuously, until just cooked through.

3. Add the Worcestershire sauce and stir.

4. Put the contents of the frying pan into a food processor, or liquidizer, and blend for ½-1 minute until just smooth.

5. Add the creamed butter and the brandy to the processor and process again until the pâté is smooth.

6. Transfer the pâté to 1 large dish, or 4 individual serving dishes, and refrigerate until required.

TIME: Preparation takes about 15 minutes and cooking a further 15 minutes.

SERVING IDEAS: Serve with buttered French bread toast or crusty brown bread.

PREPARATION: If you do not have a liquidizer or food processor, the cooked chicken livers can be pressed through a wire sieve, using the back of a spoon, into a bowl; then beat in the butter and brandy to achieve the creamed pâté mixture.

COOK'S TIP: This pâté can be prepared in advance, but if you are not eating it straight away, seal the surface with clarified butter and refrigerate until required.

CHICKEN WITH APPLE CREAM SAUCE

*Fresh tasting apples and tender chicken makes this
recipe ideal for serving as part of a special meal.*

SERVES 4

60g/2oz unsalted butter
2 tbsps vegetable oil
8 skinned and boned chicken breasts
60ml/4 tbsps brandy
2 dessert apples, peeled, cored and
    coarsely chopped
1 shallot, finely chopped
1 stick celery, chopped
½ tsp dried thyme, crumbled
90ml/6 tbsps chicken stock
2 eggs, lightly beaten
90ml/6 tbsps double cream

---

1. Melt half the butter and all of the oil in a large sauté pan until it is foaming.

2. Add the chicken and fry gently, turning once or twice, until each piece is well browned.

3. Pour off most of the fat from the pan, leaving just the chicken pieces and their juices to cook.

4. Pour the brandy into the pan with the chicken and heat gently. Carefully ignite the brandy with a match and shake the sauté pan until the flames subside.

5. In a small saucepan or frying pan, melt the remaining butter. Stir in the chopped apple, shallot and celery. Cook for about 5 minutes, until soft, but not brown.

6. Add the cooked apples to the chicken portions, along with the thyme and stock. Bring the chicken to the boil, cover, reduce the heat and simmer for 30 minutes.

7. Remove the chicken from the pan and arrange on a serving dish. Put the eggs and cream into a bowl and gradually whisk in some of the hot sauce from the sauté pan. Continue whisking until all the hot sauce has been added and the mixture is smooth.

8. Return the sauce to the sauté pan and heat gently over a low temperature for 2-3 minutes, stirring constantly until the sauce thickens. Pour the hot sauce over the chicken breasts and serve garnished with some watercress.

TIME: Preparation takes 25-30 minutes, cooking takes 40-50 minutes.

PREPARATION: If preferred, the sauce can be blended using a food processor or liquidiser instead of whisking by hand.

SERVING IDEA: Serve with sauté potatoes and petit pois.

WATCHPOINT: Take great care not to allow the sauce to boil once the egg and cream is added or it will curdle.

CRUMB FRIED CHICKEN

*This dish has a slightly misleading name
since most of the "frying" is done in the oven!*

SERVES 6

1.5kg/3lb chicken
120g/4oz breadcrumbs
60g/2oz Parmesan cheese
¼ tsp powdered ginger
2 eggs, mixed with a pinch of salt
3 tbsps oil
60g/4 tbsps butter or margarine
Lemons and parsley for garnish

---

1. Preheat the oven to 200°C/400°F/Gas Mark 6. To joint the chicken, first cut off the legs, bending them backwards to break the ball and socket joint. Cut in between the ball and socket joint to completely remove the legs.

2. Cut down the breastbone with sharp poultry shears to separate the two halves. Use the poultry shears to cut through the rib cage. Use the notch in the shears to separate the wing joints from the back.

3. Cut the quarters into two pieces each. Use a sharp knife to separate the drumstick from the thigh. Cut the breasts in half, leaving some of the white meat attached to the wing joint. Cut through the bones with poultry shears.

4. Mix the breadcrumbs, Parmesan cheese and powdered ginger together. First dip the chicken into the egg and then coat with the crumbs.

5. Heat the oil in a large frying pan or sauté pan and add the butter. When hot, add the chicken, skin side down first. Cook both sides until golden brown.

6. Transfer with a slotted spoon to a baking sheet and place in the oven for 20-30 minutes, or until the juices run clear when the chicken is tested with a fork. Serve garnished with small bunches of parsley and lemon slices.

TIME: Preparation takes about 30 minutes. If using pre-jointed chicken, allow about 15-20 minutes for preparation. Chicken will take about 10-15 minutes to brown and 20-30 minutes to finish cooking in the oven.

PREPARATION: Mix the crumbs, cheese and ginger on a sheet of greaseproof paper. Place the chicken on the crumbs and shake the paper from side to side to coat easily and completely.

VARIATION: If desired, leave out the Parmesan cheese and ginger and add extra breadcrumbs, paprika, salt, pepper and a pinch of thyme.

CHICKEN GUMBO

*This African influenced dish is a soup-stew
which takes its name from the African word for okra.*

SERVES 4-6

1.5kg/3lbs chicken, cut into 6-8 pieces
120ml/4 fl oz oil
120g/4oz flour
2-3 dried red chilli peppers or 1-2 fresh
   chilli peppers
1 large onion, finely chopped
1 large green pepper, roughly chopped
3 sticks celery, finely chopped
2 cloves garlic, crushed
225g/8oz andouille sausage or garlic
   sausage, diced
1 litre/2 pints chicken stock
1 bay leaf
Salt and pepper
Dash Tabasco
120g/4oz fresh okra
Cooked long-grain rice

1. Heat the oil in a large sauté pan or frying pan and brown the chicken on both sides, 3-4 pieces at a time. Transfer the chicken to a plate and set it aside.

2. Lower the heat under the pan and add the flour. Cook over a very low heat for about 30 minutes, stirring constantly until the flour turns a rich, dark brown. Take the pan off the heat occasionally, so that the flour does not burn.

3. Add the chilli peppers, onion, green pepper, celery, garlic and sausage to the roux and cook for about 5 minutes over very low heat, stirring continuously.

4. Pour on the stock and stir well. Add the bay leaf, seasoning and a dash of Tabasco, if desired, and return the chicken to the pan. Cover and cook for about 30 minutes or until the chicken is tender.

5. Top and tail the okra and cut each part into 2-3 pieces. If okra is small, leave whole. Add to the chicken and cook for a further 10-15 minutes. Remove the bay leaf and serve the Gumbo over rice.

TIME: Preparation takes about 30 minutes and cooking takes about 1 hour 25 minutes.

VARIATION: Gumbo may also be made with prawns, pork or pigeon.

COOK'S TIP: A roux may be made ahead of time and kept in the refrigerator to use whenever needed. If the roux is cold, heat the liquid before adding.

CHICKEN FRICASÉE

Food in the Rhine Valley shows a considerable French influence while still retaining its own distinctive character, as shown in this fricasée with German cheese topping.

SERVES 6

1.5kg/3lb chicken
1 stick celery, chopped
2 carrots, chopped
1 turnip, peeled and chopped
1 small onion, finely chopped
Water to cover
Pinch salt and pepper
2 tbsps butter
2 tbsps flour
1 can artichoke hearts, drained and halved
1 egg yolk
225ml/8 fl oz cream
Salt, pepper and a pinch nutmeg
30g/1oz Tilsit cheese, thinly sliced
1 tbsp chopped fresh parsley

1. Place the chicken in a large stock pot with the vegetables and enough water to cover. Cook over medium heat for about 1 hour, or until the chicken is tender and juices run clear when the thigh is pierced with a fork.

2. Remove the chicken and allow to cool. Strain the stock and reserve it. Keep the vegetables to add to the sauce. When the chicken is cool, skin it and remove the meat from the bones. Discard the skin and bones and chop the meat roughly.

3. Melt the butter in a large pan and stir in the flour off the heat. Place the pan back over low heat and cook until the flour is a pale straw colour. Pour in about 570ml/1 pint of the strained stock gradually. Whisk well and bring the sauce to the boil. Add the chicken, reserved vegetables and the artichoke hearts. Cook for about 10 minutes over low heat and then remove to a heated serving dish with a draining spoon.

4. Mix the egg and cream together and combine with a few spoonfuls of the hot sauce. Put the egg and cream back to the sauce and stir well. Heat gently, but do not allow to boil. Season with salt, pepper and nutmeg, and pour over chicken.

5. Cut the cheese into strips or triangles and arrange attractively on top. Place under a preheated grill to brown the cheese. Sprinkle with the chopped parsley and serve immediately.

TIME: Preparation takes about 20 minutes, cooking takes about 1 hour 15 minutes.

FREEZING: Any leftover stock may be frozen.

WATCHPOINT: Do not allow the sauce to boil once the egg and cream have been added or the mixture will curdle.

CHICKEN WITH BLACKCURRANT SAUCE

*The sharp tang of blackcurrants makes an ideal
partner for lightly cooked chicken.*

SERVES 4

4 chicken breasts, boned and skinned
Salt
3 tbsps sesame oil
225g/8oz fresh blackcurrants
Juice of 1 orange
140ml/¼ pint red wine
Artificial sweetener, to taste
Orange slices and fresh blackcurrants
   to garnish

1. Season the chicken breasts with a little salt. Heat the oil in a shallow frying pan.

2. Gently fry the chicken breasts for 4-5 minutes on each side, until they are golden brown and tender.

3. Top and tail the blackcurrants and put them into a small pan, along with the orange juice and red wine. Bring to the boil, then cover and simmer gently until the blackcurrants are soft.

4. Using a liquidiser or food processor, blend the blackcurrants and the cooking juice for 30 seconds.

5. Rub the blended purée through a nylon sieve with the back of a spoon, pressing the fruit through to reserve all the juice and pulp but leaving the pips in the sieve.

6. Put the sieved purée into a small saucepan with the sweetener and heat gently, stirring constantly until the liquid has reduced and the sauce is thick and smooth.

7. Arrange the chicken breasts on a serving dish, and spoon the blackcurrant sauce over. Garnish with orange slices and fresh blackcurrants.

TIME: Preparation takes 15 minutes, cooking takes approximately 15 minutes.

VARIATION: Use blackberries instead of blackcurrants in this recipe.

PREPARATION: To test if the chicken breasts are cooked, insert a skewer into the thickest part then press gently. If the juices run clear, the meat is cooked.

SERVING IDEA: Serve with a selection of fresh green vegetables.

19

CHICKEN AND SAUSAGE RISOTTO

This is really a one pot meal and one you won't have to cook in the oven.

SERVES 4-6

1.5kg/3lbs chicken skinned,
   boned, and cut into cubes
3 tbsps butter or margarine
1 large onion, roughly chopped
3 sticks celery, roughly chopped
1 large green pepper, seeded and
   roughly chopped
1 clove garlic, crushed
Salt and pepper
225g/8oz uncooked rice
400g/14oz tinned tomatoes
180g/6oz smoked sausage, cut into
   1.25cm/½ inch dice
850ml/1½ pints chicken stock
Chopped parsley

1. Use the chicken bones, skin, onion and celery trimming to make stock. Cover the ingredients with water, bring to the boil and then simmer slowly for 1 hour. Strain liquid and reserve.

2. Melt the butter or margarine in a large saucepan and add the onion. Cook slowly to brown and then add the celery, green pepper and garlic and cook briefly.

3. Add the salt and pepper and the rice, stirring to mix well.

4. Add the chicken, tomatoes, sausage and stock and mix well. Bring to the boil, then reduce the heat to simmering and cook about 20-25 minutes, stirring occasionally until the chicken is done and the rice is tender. The rice should have absorbed most of the liquid by the time it has cooked. Garnish with chopped parsley before serving.

TIME: Preparation takes about 35-40 minutes and cooking takes about 20-25 minutes.

PREPARATION: Check the level of liquid occasionally as the rice is cooking and add more water or stock as necessary. If there is a lot of liquid left and the rice is nearly cooked, uncover the pan and boil rapidly.

SERVING IDEAS: Add a green salad to make a complete meal.

CHICKEN POLISH STYLE

Choose small, young chickens for a truly Polish-style dish.
A dried white roll was originally used for stuffing,
but breadcrumbs are easier.

SERVES 4

2 chickens, weighing approximately
    900g/2lbs each
2 chicken livers
1 tbsp butter or margarine
6 slices bread, made into crumbs
2 tsps chopped parsley
1 tsp chopped dill
1 egg
Salt and pepper
140ml/¼ pint chicken stock

1. Remove the fat from just inside the cavities of the chickens and discard it. Melt the butter in a small frying pan. Pick over the chicken livers and cut away any discoloured portions. Add chicken livers to the butter and cook until just brown. Chop and set aside.

2. Combine the breadcrumbs, herbs, egg, salt and pepper and mix well. Mix in the chopped chicken livers.

3. Stuff the cavities of the chickens with the breadcrumb mixture and sew up the openings. Tie the legs together.

4. Place the chickens in a roasting pan and spread the breasts and legs thinly with butter. Pour the stock around the chickens and roast in a preheated 190°C/ 375°F/Gas Mark 5 oven for about 40-45 minutes. Baste frequently with the pan juices during roasting.

5. To check if the chickens are done, pierce the thickest part of the thigh with a skewer or small, sharp knife. If the juices run clear the chickens are ready. If the juices are pink, return to the oven for another 5-10 minutes.

6. When the chickens are done, remove them from the roasting pan, remove the strings and keep the chickens warm. Skim any fat from the surface of the pan juices. If a lot of liquid has accumulated, pour into a small saucepan and reduce over high heat. Pour the juices over the chicken to serve.

TIME: Preparation takes about 20 minutes and cooking takes about 45 minutes.

VARIATION: Chopped mushrooms or onions may be added to the stuffing, if desired.

CHICKEN MOGHLAI WITH CORIANDER CHUTNEY

*The creamy spiciness of the chicken is a good
contrast to the hotness of the chutney.*

SERVES 4-6

60ml/4 tbsps oil
1.5kg/3lbs chicken pieces, skinned
1 tsp ground cardamom
½ tsp ground cinnamon
1 bay leaf
4 cloves
2 onions, finely chopped
2.5cm/1-inch piece fresh ginger, grated
4 cloves garlic, crushed
30g/1oz ground almonds
2 tbsps cumin seeds
Pinch cayenne pepper
280ml/½ pint single cream
6 tbsps natural yogurt
2 tbsps roasted cashew nuts
2 tbsps sultanas

Chutney
90g/3oz fresh coriander leaves
1 green chilli pepper, chopped and seeded
1 tbsp lemon juice
Salt and pepper
Pinch sugar
1 tbsp oil
½ tsp ground coriander

1. To prepare the chicken, heat the oil in a large frying pan. Fry the chicken pieces on each side until golden brown.

2. Remove the chicken and set aside. Add the cardamom, cinnamon, bay leaf and cloves to the hot oil and meat juices and fry for 30 seconds. Stir in the onions and fry until soft but not brown.

3. Stir the ginger, garlic, almonds, cumin and cayenne pepper into the onions. Cook gently for 2-3 minutes, then stir in the cream.

4. Return the chicken pieces to the pan, along with any juices. Cover and simmer gently for 30-40 minutes, or until the chicken is cooked and tender.

5. Whilst the chicken is cooking, prepare the chutney. Put the coriander leaves, chilli, lemon juice, seasoning and sugar into a blender or food processor and work to a paste.

6. Heat the oil, add the ground coriander and cook for 1 minute. Add this mixture to the processed coriander leaves and blend in thoroughly.

7. Just before serving, stir the yogurt, cashews and sultanas into the chicken. Heat through just enough to plump up the sultanas, but do not allow the mixture to boil.

8. Serve at once with the coriander chutney.

TIME: Preparation takes about 25 minutes, and cooking takes 30-40 minutes.

SERVING IDEAS: Serve with boiled rice and a cucumber and tomato salad.

CHICKEN MONTEREY

*There's a touch of Mexican flavour in this
chicken recipe with its accompaniment
of colourful and spicy salsa.*

SERVES 6

6 boned chicken breasts
Grated rind and juice of 1 lime
2 tbsps olive oil
Coarsely ground black pepper
90ml/6 tbsps whole grain mustard
2 tsps paprika
4 ripe tomatoes, peeled, seeded and
    quartered
2 shallots, chopped
1 clove garlic, crushed
½ Jalapeño pepper or other chilli pepper,
    seeded and chopped
1 tsp wine vinegar
Pinch salt
2 tbsps chopped fresh coriander
Whole coriander leaves to garnish

1. Place chicken breasts in a shallow dish with the lime rind and juice, oil, pepper, mustard and paprika. Marinate for about 1 hour, turning occasionally.

2. To peel tomatoes, drop them into boiling water for about 5 seconds or less depending on ripeness. Place immediately in cold water. The peels should now come off easily.

3. Place tomatoes, shallots, garlic, chilli pepper, vinegar and salt in a food processor or blender and process until coarsely chopped. Stir in the coriander by hand. Set aside.

4. Remove the chicken from the marinade, place on a grill pan and reserve the marinade. Cook chicken skin side uppermost for about 7-10 minutes, depending on how close the chicken is to the heat source. Baste frequently with the remaining marinade. Grill other side in the same way. Sprinkle with salt after grilling.

5. Place chicken on serving plates and garnish top with coriander leaves or sprigs. Serve with the tomato salsa on one side.

TIME: Preparation takes about 1 hour and cooking takes 14-20 minutes.

PREPARATION: Salsa can be prepared in advance and kept in the refrigerator. It can also be served with other poultry, meat or seafood. It also makes a good dip for vegetable crudités or tortilla chips.

WATCHPOINT: When preparing chilli peppers, wear rubber gloves or at least be sure to wash hands thoroughly after handling them. Do not touch eyes or face before washing hands.

GREEN GODDESS SALAD

*Chicken, anchovies and avocado combine in
this fresh recipe named for its green dressing.*

SERVES 4

8 anchovy fillets, soaked in milk, rinsed
    and dried
1 spring onion, chopped
2 tbsps chopped fresh tarragon
3 tbsps chopped chives
60g/4 tbsps chopped parsley
280ml/½ pint prepared mayonnaise
140ml/¼ pint natural yogurt
2 tbsps tarragon vinegar
Pinch sugar and cayenne pepper
1 large head lettuce
450g/1lb cooked chicken
1 avocado, peeled and sliced or cubed
1 tbsp lemon juice

1. Combine all the ingredients, except the
lettuce, avocado and chicken and lemon
juice, in a food processor. Work the
ingredients until smooth, well mixed and
green. Leave in the refrigerator at least 1
hour for the flavours to blend.

2. Shred the lettuce or tear into bite-size
pieces and arrange on plates.

3. Top the lettuce with the cooked
chicken cut into strips or cubes.

4. Spoon the dressing over the chicken.
Brush the avocado slices or toss the cubes
with lemon juice and garnish the salad.
Serve any remaining dressing separately.

TIME: Preparation takes about 30 minutes.

PREPARATION: The dressing may be prepared ahead of time and kept in the
refrigerator for a day or two.

SERVING IDEAS: The dressing may be served as a dip for vegetable crudités
or with a tossed salad.

CHICKEN AND CASHEW NUTS

*Many oriental dishes are stir-fried. This
simply means the ingredients being stirred
continuously to prevent them from burning.*

SERVES 4

340g/12oz chicken breast meat, sliced into
   2.5cm/1-inch pieces
1 tbsp cornflour
1 tsp salt
1 tsp sesame oil
1 tbsp light soy sauce
½ tsp sugar
75ml/5 tbsps vegetable oil
2 spring onions, trimmed and chopped
1 small onion, diced
2.5cm/1-inch piece fresh root ginger,
   peeled and finely sliced
2 cloves garlic, finely sliced
90g/3oz mange tout
60g/2oz bamboo shoots, thinly sliced
120g/4oz cashew nuts
2 tsps cornflour
1 tbsp hoisin sauce, or barbecue sauce
250ml/9 fl oz chicken stock

1. Roll the chicken pieces in the cornflour.
Reserve any excess cornflour.

2. Mix together the salt, sesame oil, soy
sauce and sugar in a large mixing boil. Put
the chicken into this marinade mixture
and leave to stand in a refrigerator for 10
minutes.

3. Heat 2 tbsps vegetable oil in a large
wok and stir-fry the onions, ginger and
garlic for 2-3 minutes.

4. Add the mange tout and the bamboo
shoots to the onion mixture. Stir-fry for a
further 3 minutes.

5. Remove the fried vegetables and
reserve. Add a further 1 tbsp oil to the
wok and heat through.

6. Lift the chicken pieces out of the
marinade and stir-fry these in the hot oil
for 3-4 minutes, until cooked through.

7. Remove the cooked chicken pieces and
clean the wok.

8. Add the remaining oil and return the
chicken and fried vegetables to the wok,
and stir in the cashew nuts.

9. Mix together the remaining cornflour,
the hoisin or barbecue sauce and the
chicken stock. Pour this over the chicken
and vegetables in the wok and cook over
a moderate heat, stirring continuously,
until the ingredients are heated through
and the sauce has thickened.

TIME: Preparation takes about 15 minutes and cooking takes about 15 minutes.

VARIATION: Stir 90g/3oz pineapple chunks into the stir-fry mixture just before serving.

SERVING IDEAS: Serve this stir-fry with a dish of Chinese noodles.

31

CHICKEN POT PIE

*Not a true pie, this dish is nevertheless warming winter fare
with its creamy sauce and puffy biscuit topping.*

SERVES 4

4 chicken joints, 2 breasts and 2 legs
1.5ltr/2½ pints water
1 bay leaf
2 sprigs thyme
1 sprig rosemary
1 sprig fresh tarragon or ¼ tsp dry tarragon
4 whole peppercorns
1 allspice berry
90ml/4 tbsps white wine
2 carrots, peeled and diced
24 pearl onions, peeled
6 tbsps frozen corn kernels
140ml/¼ pint double cream
Salt

Biscuit Topping
400g/14oz plain flour
1½ tbsps baking powder
Pinch salt
75g/5 tbsps butter or margarine
340ml/12fl oz milk
1 egg, beaten with a pinch of salt

1. Place the chicken in a deep saucepan with water, herbs and spices and wine. Cover and bring to the boil. Reduce the heat and allow to simmer for 20-30 minutes, or until the chicken is tender. Remove the chicken from the pot and allow to cool. Skim and dicard the fat from the surface of the stock. Skin the chicken and remove the meat from the bones.

2. Continue to simmer the stock until reduced by about half. Strain the stock and add the carrots and onions. Cook until tender and add the corn. Stir in the cream and add the chicken meat. Pour into a casserole or into individual baking dishes.

3. To prepare the topping, sift the dry ingredients into a bowl or place them in a food processor and process once or twice to sift.

4. Rub in the butter or margarine until the mixture resembles small peas. Stir in enough of the milk until the mixture comes together.

5. Turn out onto a floured surface and knead lightly. Roll out with a floured rolling pin and cut with a pastry cutter. Brush the surface of each biscuit with a mixture of egg and salt. Place the biscuit on top of the chicken mixture and bake for 10-15 minutes in a preheated oven at 190°C/375°F/Gas Mark 5. Serve immediately.

TIME: Preparation takes about 25 minutes and cooking takes about 20-30 minutes for the chicken, about 20 minutes to prepare the sauce, and about 10-15 minutes to finish the dish.

VARIATIONS: Diced potatoes may be added to the sauce along with other vegetables. Add chopped fresh parsley or a pinch of dried thyme as well, if desired.

CHICKEN ST. PIERRE

*A French name for a delicious combination
of chicken, broad beans, peppers and onions
made into a spicy, aromatic stew.*

SERVES 4-6

1.5kg/3lbs chicken, cut in 8 pieces
90g/6 tbsps butter or margarine
3 tbsps flour
1 large red pepper, diced
1 large green pepper, diced
6 spring onions, chopped
140ml/¼ pint dry white wine
280ml/½ pint chicken stock
180g/6oz broad beans
1 tsp chopped thyme
Salt, pepper and pinch nutmeg
Dash Tabasco (optional)

1. To cut the chicken in 8 pieces, remove the legs first by cutting between the legs and the body of the chicken.

2. Bend the legs backwards to break the joint and cut away from the body.

3. Cut the drumstick and thigh joints in half.

4. Cut down the breastbone with a sharp knife and then use poultry shears to cut through the bone and ribcage to remove the breast joints from the back.

5. Cut both breast joints in half, leaving some white meat attached to the wing joint.

6. Heat the butter in a large sauté pan and, when foaming, add the chicken pieces, skin side down. Brown on one side, turn over and brown other side. Remove the chicken and keep warm. Add the flour to the pan and cook to a pale straw colour. Add the peppers and onions and cook briefly.

7. Add the wine and chicken stock and bring to the boil, stirring constantly until thickened. Add the chicken, broad beans, thyme, seasoning and nutmeg. Cover the pan and cook for about 25 minutes, or until the chicken is tender. Add Tabasco to taste, if desired, before serving.

TIME: Preparation takes about 35 minutes and cooking takes about 40 minutes.

PREPARATION: For crisper vegetables, add them after the chicken and sauce have cooked for about 15 minutes.

FREEZING: Chicken can be prepared in advance and reheated or frozen for up to three months. Thaw completely before reheating.

LIME-ROASTED CHICKEN

*This simply made, but unusual, main course is
very low in calories and high in tangy flavour.*

SERVES 4

4 chicken breast portions, each weighing
  about 225g/8oz
Salt and freshly ground black pepper
4 limes
2 tsps white wine vinegar
75ml/5 tbsps olive oil
2 tsp fresh chopped basil

1. Rub the chicken portions all over with salt and black pepper. Place in a shallow ovenproof dish, and set aside.

2. Carefully pare away thin strips of the rind only from 2 of the limes and reserve. Cut these 2 limes in half and squeeze the juice.

3. Add the lime juice to the vinegar and 4 tbsps of the olive oil in a small dish, along with the strips of rind, and mix well.

4. Pour the oil and lime juice mixture over the chicken portions in the dish. Cover and refrigerate for about 4 hours or overnight.

5. Remove the covering from the dish in which the chicken is marinating, and baste the chicken well with the marinade mixture. Place in a preheated oven 190°C/375°F/Gas Mark 5 and cook for 30-35 minutes, or until the chicken is well roasted and tender.

6. In the meantime, peel away the rind and white pith from the 2 remaining limes and discard. Cut the limes into thin slices using a sharp knife.

7. Heat the remaining oil in a small frying pan and add the lime slices and basil. Cook quickly for 1 minute, or until the fragrance rises up from the basil and the limes just begin to soften.

8. Serve the chicken portions on a serving platter, garnished with the fried lime slices and a little extra fresh basil, if desired.

TIME: Preparation takes 25 minutes, plus 4 hours marinating time.
Cooking takes 40 minutes.

WATCHPOINT: Puncture the chicken with a skewer at its thickest point
and when the resulting juices run clear, it is ready.

VARIATION: Use lemons instead of limes, and thyme instead of basil.

PREPARATION: The chicken can be prepared in advance and marinated overnight.

CHICKEN TOMATO

Made with a very fragrant selection of spices,
this dish is sure to become a firm favourite.

SERVES 4-6

1 onion, peeled and chopped
3 tbsps oil
2.5cm/1-inch piece cinnamon stick
1 bay leaf
6 cloves
Seeds of 6 small cardamoms
2.5cm/1-inch piece fresh ginger, grated
4 cloves garlic, crushed
1.5kg/3lb roasting chicken, cut into
    8-10 pieces
1 tsp chilli powder
1 tsp ground cumin
1 tsp ground coriander
400g/14oz tinned tomatoes, chopped
1 tsp salt
2 sprigs fresh coriander leaves, chopped
2 green chillies, halved seeded, and
    chopped

1. In a large saucepan, fry the onion in the oil, until it has softened. Add the cinnamon, bay leaf, cloves, cardamom seeds, ginger and garlic. Fry for 1 minute.

2. Add the chicken pieces to the saucepan. Sprinkle the chilli powder, ground cumin and coriander over the chicken and fry for a further 2 minutes, stirring continuously, to ensure the spices do not burn.

3. Stir in the remaining ingredients, mixing well to blend the spices evenly. Cover the pan and simmer for 40-45 minutes, or until the chicken is tender. Remove the cinnamon stick and bay leaf before serving.

TIME: Preparation takes about 30 minutes, and cooking takes about 40-50 minutes.

PREPARATION: If you ask your butcher, he will joint the chicken for you.

SERVING IDEAS: Serve with boiled rice.

FRIED CHICKEN CREOLE

*Not the usual crisp Southern-style fried chicken, this is cooked
in a tomato sauce flavoured with garlic, herbs and wine.*

SERVES 6

1.5kg/3lbs frying chicken, cut into serving
  pieces
Flour for dredging
Salt and pepper
90ml/6 tbsps oil
75g/5 tbsps butter or margarine
1 small onion, finely chopped
1 clove garlic, crushed
120g/4oz streaky bacon or gammon, diced
6 tomatoes, peeled and chopped
2 tsps fresh thyme or 1 tsp dried thyme
140ml/¼ pint white wine
2 tbsps chopped parsley

1. Mix the flour with salt and pepper and
dredge the chicken lightly, shaking the
pieces to remove any excess flour. Heat
the oil in a large sauté pan or frying pan
and, when hot, add the butter.

2. Add the chicken drumsticks and thigh
pieces skin side down and allow to
brown. Turn the pieces over and brown
on the other side. Brown over moderately
low heat so that the chicken cooks as well
as browns. Push the chicken to one side
of the pan, add the breast meat, and
brown in the same way.

3. Add the onion, garlic and bacon or
gammon to the pan and lower the heat.
Cook slowly for about 10 minutes, or until
the bacon browns slightly. Add the
tomatoes and thyme and lower the heat.
Cook until the chicken is just tender and
the tomatoes are softened.

4. Using a draining spoon, transfer the
chicken and other ingredients to a serving
dish and keep warm. Remove all but
about 4 tbsps of the fat from the pan and
mix in the wine, scraping up the browned
bits from the bottom. Bring to the boil and
allow to reduce slightly. Pour over the
chicken to serve, and sprinkle with
chopped parsley.

TIME: Preparation takes about 25 minutes and cooking takes about 30-40 minutes.

PREPARATION: Brown the chicken slowly so that it cooks at the same time as it browns.
This will cut down on the length of cooking time once all the ingredients are added.

TARRAGON CHICKEN PANCAKES

*These attractive pancakes look sophisticated enough for a dinner party,
but are so easy to make, you can indulge yourself at any time.*

SERVES 4

120g/4oz plain wholemeal flour
1 egg
280ml/½ pint skimmed milk
Polynsaturated vegetable oil, for frying
45g/1½ oz plain unbleached flour
280ml/½ pint skimmed milk
Freshly ground sea salt and black pepper,
   to taste
225g/8oz cooked chicken, chopped
1 avocado pear, peeled, halved, stoned
   and chopped
2 tsps lemon juice
1 tbsp chopped fresh tarragon

---

1. Put the wholemeal flour into a large bowl, and make a slight well in the centre. Break the egg into the well and begin to beat the egg carefully into the flour, incorporating only a little flour at a time.

2. Add the milk gradually to the egg and flour mixture, beating well between additions, until all the milk is incorporated and the batter is smooth.

3. Heat a little oil in a small frying pan, or crêpe pan, and cook about 2 tbsps of the batter at a time, tipping and rotating the pan, so that the batter spreads evenly over the base to form a pancake. Flip the pancake over to cook the second side.

4. Repeat this process until all the batter has been used up. Keep the pancakes warm until required.

5. Blend the plain flour with a little of the remaining skimmed milk, and gradually add the rest of the milk, until it is all incorporated.

6. Pour the flour and milk mixture into a small pan, and cook over a moderate heat, stirring continuously, until the sauce has thickened. Season to taste.

7. Stir the chopped chicken, avocado, lemon juice and tarragon into the sauce.

8. Fold each pancake in half, and then in half again, to form a triangle.

9. Carefully open part of the triangle out to form an envelope, and fill this with the chicken and avocado mixture.

TIME: Preparation takes about 25 minutes, and cooking takes about 25 minutes.

PREPARATION: Use 280ml/½ pint 1% fat fromage frais, instead of the skimmed milk, for a luxurious change to this recipe.

SERVING IDEAS: Serve piping hot, garnished with watercress and a crisp green salad.

COUNTRY CAPTAIN CHICKEN

*A flavourful dish named for a sea captain with
a taste for the spicy cuisine of India.*

SERVES 6

1.5kg/3lbs chicken portions
Seasoned flour
90ml/6 tbsps oil
1 medium onion, chopped
1 medium green pepper, seeded
   and chopped
1 clove garlic, crushed
Pinch salt and pepper
2 tsps curry powder
2 14oz cans tomatoes
2 tsps chopped parsley
1 tsp chopped marjoram
60g/4 tbsps currants or raisins
120g/4oz blanched almond halves

1. Remove skin from the chicken and dredge with flour, shaking off the excess. Heat the oil and brown the chicken on all sides until golden. Remove to an ovenproof casserole.

2. Pour off all but about 2 tbsps of the oil. Add the onion, pepper and garlic and cook slowly to soften. Add the seasoning and curry powder and cook, stirring frequently, for 2 minutes.

3. Add the tomatoes, parsley, majoram and bring to the boil. Pour the sauce over the chicken, cover and cook in a pre-heated 350°F oven for 45 minutes.

4. Add the currants or raisins during the last 15 minutes. Meanwhile, toast the almonds in the oven on a baking sheet along with the chicken. Stir them carefully and watch carefully. Sprinkle over the chicken just before serving.

TIME: Preparation takes 30 minutes, cooking takes about 50 minutes.

CHICKEN TIKKA

*Red food colouring gives this dish its
traditional appearance, but the taste will not
be affected if you prefer not to use it.*

SERVES 4-6

140ml/¼ pint natural yogurt
1 tsp chilli powder
2 tsps ginger paste
2 tsps garlic paste
2 tsps garam masala
½ tsp salt
¼ tsp red food colouring
Juice of 1 lemon
1.5kg/3lb roasting chicken, cut into
   8-10 pieces
Oil for brushing

1. In a large bowl, mix together the yogurt, chilli powder, ginger and garlic pastes, garam masala, salt, colouring and lemon juice.

2. Add the chicken pieces to the yogurt mixture and mix in well to ensure they are evenly coated.

3. Line a grill pan with aluminium foil and arrange the chicken pieces on this, together with the yogurt sauce. Preheat the grill to moderate and grill the chicken pieces for about 5-6 minutes on each side, brushing with a little oil if necessary, to prevent them burning. Pierce the thickest part of the chicken pieces with a skewer, if the juices run clear the chicken is ready if the juices are still pink, return to the grill for a few more minutes.

TIME: Preparation takes about 10 minutes, and cooking takes about 30 minutes.

PREPARATION: On request, most butchers will cut the chicken into pieces for you.

VARIATION: Use chicken drumsticks instead of a whole cut chicken.

SERVING IDEAS: Serve with wedges of lemon and a crisp lettuce and tomato salad.

CHICKEN WITH AUBERGINE AND SMOKED HAM STUFFING

*Aubergine and ham make an unusual stuffing
and add interest to roast chicken.*

SERVES 4-6

1.5kg/3lb roasting chicken
1 small aubergine
2 tbsps butter or margarine
1 small onion, finely chopped
120g/4oz ham, chopped
120g/4oz fresh breadcrumbs
2 tsps chopped mixed herbs
Salt and pepper
1-2 eggs, beaten
2 tbsps additional butter, softened

1. Cut the aubergine in half lengthways and remove stem. Lightly score the surface with a sharp knife and sprinkle with salt. Leave to stand for about 30 minutes for the salt to draw out any bitter juices.

2. Melt 2 tbsps butter in a medium saucepan and when foaming, add the onion. Cook slowly to soften slightly.

3. Rinse the aubergine and pat dry. Cut into ½ inch cubes. Cook with the onion until fairly soft. Add the ham, breadcrumbs, herbs and seasoning and beat in the egg gradually until the mixture just holds together. Add salt and pepper to taste.

4. Remove the fat from just inside the chicken cavity. Fill the neck end with the stuffing. Place any extra in a greased casserole.

5. Tuck the wing tips under the chicken to hold the neck flap down. Tie the legs together and place the chicken in a roasting pan. Spread over the remaining softened butter and roast in a preheated 180°C/350°F/Gas Mark 4 oven for about 1 hour, or until the juices from the chicken run clear when the thickest part of the chicken is pierced with a sharp knife.

6. Cook the extra stuffing, covered for the last 35 minutes of cooking time. Leave the chicken to stand for 10 minutes before carving. If desired, make a gravy with the pan juices.

TIME: Preparation takes about 30 minutes and cooking takes about 50 minutes for the stuffing and about 1 hour for the chicken.

VARIATION: Other ingredients, such as chopped red or green peppers, celery or spring onions, may be added to the stuffing.

WATCHPOINT: Do not stuff the chicken until ready to cook.

CHICKEN CACCIATORE

The use of herbs, wine and vinegar in this
delicious Italian family meal gives a wonderful,
hearty flavour without the need for salt.

SERVES 4-6

60ml/4 tbsps olive oil
1.5kg/3lbs chicken pieces
2 onions, sliced
3 cloves garlic, crushed
225g/8oz buttom mushrooms, quartered
140ml/¼ pint red wine
1 tbsp wine vinegar
1 tbsp fresh chopped parsley
2 tsps fresh chopped oregano
2 tsps fresh chopped basil
1 bay leaf
450g/1lb tinned tomatoes
140ml/¼ pint chicken stock
Freshly ground black pepper
Pinch of sugar

1. In a large frying pan heat the oil and lay the chicken pieces, skin side down, in one layer.

2. Brown for 3-4 minutes, then turn each piece over. Continue turning the chicken portions until all surfaces are well browned.

3. Remove the chicken portions to a plate and keep warm.

4. Add the onions and garlic to the oil and chicken juices in the frying pan. Cook lightly for 2-3 minutes, or until they are just beginning to brown.

5. Add the mushrooms to the pan and cook for about 1 minute, stirring constantly.

6. Pour the wine and vinegar into the pan and boil rapidly to reduce to about half the original quantity.

7. Add the herbs, bay leaf and tomatoes, stirring well to break up the tomatoes.

8. Stir in the chicken stock and season with pepper and sugar.

9. Return the chicken to the tomato sauce and cover with a tight fitting lid. Simmer for about 1 hour, or until the chicken is tender. Remove the bay leaf before serving.

TIME: Preparation takes about 20 minutes, cooking takes 1 hour 15 minutes.

SERVING IDEA: Serve with rice or pasta, and a mixed salad.

PECAN CHICKEN

*In America's deep South pecans are often used in
both sweet and savoury dishes. In this dish their rich,
sweet taste complements a stuffing for chicken.*

SERVES 4

---

4 boned chicken breasts
3 tbsps butter or margarine
1 small onion, finely chopped
90g/3oz pork sausage meat
90g/3oz fresh breadcrumbs
1 tsp chopped thyme
1 tsp chopped parsley
1 small egg, lightly beaten
120g/4oz pecan halves
280ml/½ pint chicken stock
1 tbsp flour
2 tbsps sherry
Salt and pepper
Chopped parsley or watercress to garnish

---

1. Cut a small pocket in the thick side of each chicken breast using a small knife.

2. Melt 1 tbsp butter in a small saucepan and add the onion. Cook for a few minutes over gentle heat to soften. Add the sausage meat and turn up the heat to brown the meat. Break up the sausage meat with a fork as it cooks.

3. Drain off any excess fat and add the breadcrumbs, herbs and a pinch of salt and pepper. Allow to cool slightly and add enough egg to hold the mixture together. Chop the pecans, reserving 8, and add to the stuffing.

4. Using a teaspoon, fill the pocket in each chicken breast with some of the stuffing.

5. Melt 1 tbsp butter in a heavy saucepan and add the chicken breasts, skin side down first. Brown over moderate heat and turn over. Brown the other side quickly to seal.

6. Pour in the stock, cover the pan and cook for about 25-30 minutes in a preheated 180°C/°350°F/Gas Mark 4 oven until tender.

7. When the chicken is cooked, remove it to a serving plate and keep warm. Reserve the cooking liquid.

8. Melt the remaining butter in a small saucepan and stir in the flour. Cook gently to a pale straw colour. Strain on the cooking liquid and add the sherry. Bring to the boil and stir constantly until thickened. Add the remaining pecans and seasoning.

9. To serve, spoon some of the sauce over the chicken and garnish with chopped parsley or watercress.

TIME: Preparation takes about 30 minutes and cooking takes about 40 minutes.

VARIATION: If pecans are unavailable, use hazelnuts. Crush the hazelnuts roughly for the garnish and brown lightly in the butter before adding flour for the sauce.

SERVING IDEAS: Serve with a combination of white and wild rice.

CHICKEN ESCALOPES

*Chicken is an excellent meat for those wishing to keep
a check on the amount of saturated fat in their diet.
This simple recipe makes the most of tender chicken breasts.*

SERVES 4

4 chicken breasts, boned and skinned
2 tbsps seasoned wholemeal flour
8 tbsps fresh wholemeal breadcrumbs
1 tbsp chopped fresh sage
1 egg, beaten
30g/1oz polynsaturated margarine
1 tbsp olive oil
75ml/5 tbsps low calorie mayonnaise
140ml/¼ pint low fat natural yogurt or
   1% fat fromage frais
1 tsp grated fresh horseradish
2 tbsps chopped shelled walnuts

1. Dust the chicken breasts lightly in the seasoned flour.

2. Mix together the wholemeal breadcrumbs and the fresh sage on a plate.

3. Dip the floured chicken breasts first into the beaten egg, and then into the sage and breadcrumb mixture, pressing the crumbs onto the chicken breasts, to make sure they are coated thoroughly.

4. Chill the chicken breasts for 30 minutes in the refrigerator.

5. Heat the margarine and oil in a large, shallow frying pan. Add the prepared chicken breasts and fry them gently on each side for 5 minutes, or until they are golden and the meat is tender and cooked.

6. Mix together the mayonnaise, yogurt, horseradish and chopped walnuts.

7. Arrange the cooked escalopes on a serving plate and pour a little of the yogurt and walnut sauce over them before serving.

TIME: Prepartion takes about 20 minutes, and cooking takes about 10-15 minutes.

VARIATION: Use chopped fresh tarragon leaves, instead of the sage.

SERVING IDEAS: Serve with new potatoes and cooked French beans.

BRUNSWICK STEW

*Peppers, potatoes, corn, tomatoes, onions and broad beans
are staple ingredients in this recipe, which once included
squirrel in its really authentic version!*

SERVES 6-8

1.5kg/3lbs chicken portions
90g/6 tbsps flour
3 tbsps butter or margarine
225g/8oz thick-sliced bacon, rinded and
    cut into ¼ inch dice
3 medium onions, finely chopped
3 pints water
3 14oz cans tomatoes
3 tbsps tomato paste
120g/4oz fresh or frozen broad beans
120g/4oz sweetcorn
2 large red peppers, seeded and cut
    into small dice
3 medium potatoes, peeled and cut
    into ½ inch cubes
Salt and pepper
1-2 tsps cayenne pepper or Tabasco,
    or to taste
2 tsps Worcestershire sauce
225ml/8fl oz red wine

1. Put the flour in a clear plastic bag, add the chicken and shake to coat the chicken thoroughly.

2. In a large, deep sauté pan, melt the butter until foaming. Add the chicken without crowding the pieces and brown over moderately high heat for about 10-12 minutes. Remove the chicken and set it aside.

3. In the same pan, fry the bacon until the fat is rendered and the dice are crisp.

4. Add the onions and cook over a moderate heat for about 10 minutes, or until softened but not browned.

5. Pour the water into a large stockpot or saucepan and spoon in the onions, bacon and any meat juices from the pan. Add the chicken, tomatoes and tomato paste. Bring to the boil, reduce the heat and simmer for about 1-1½ hours.

6. Add the broad beans, corn, peppers and potatoes. Add the cayenne pepper or Tabasco to taste. Add the Worcestershire sauce and red wine.

7. Cook for a further 30 minutes or until the chicken is tender. Add salt and pepper to taste.

8. The stew should be rather thick, if there is too much liquid, remove the chicken and vegetables and boil down the liquid to reduce it. If there is not enough liquid, add more water or chicken stock.

TIME: Preparation takes about 1 hour and cooking takes about 2 hours.

CHICKEN WITH RED PEPPERS

Easy as this recipe is, it looks and tastes good enough for guests.

SERVES 4

4 large red peppers
4 skinned and boned chicken breasts
1½ tbsps oil
Salt and pepper
1 clove garlic, finely chopped
3 tbsps white wine vinegar
2 spring onions, finely chopped
Sage leaves for garnish

1. Cut the peppers in half and remove the stems, cores and seeds. Flatten the peppers with the palm of your hand and brush the skin sides lightly with oil.

2. Place the peppers skin side up on the rack of a preheated grill and cook about 5cm/2 inches away from the heat source until the skins are well blistered and charred.

3. Wrap the peppers in a clean towel and allow them to stand until cool. Peel off the skins with a small vegetable knife. Cut into thin strips and set aside.

4. Place the chicken breasts between two sheets of dampened greaseproof paper and flatten by hitting with a rolling pin or meat mallet.

5. Heat the oil in a large frying pan. Season the chicken breasts on both sides and place in the hot oil. Cook 5 minutes, turn over and cook until tender and lightly browned. Remove the chicken and keep it warm.

6. Add the pepper strips, garlic, vinegar and spring onions to the pan and cook briefly until the vinegar loses its strong aroma.

7. Place the chicken breasts on serving plates. Spoon over the pan juices.

8. Arrange the pepper mixture with the chicken and garnish with the sage leaves.

TIME: Preparation takes about 35-40 minutes and cooking takes about 10 minutes to char the peppers and about 20 minutes to finish the dish.

BUYING GUIDE: If fresh sage is unavailable, substitute coriander or parsley leaves as a garnish.

DICED CHICKEN AND PEPPERS

This spicy and colourful Chinese dish has the added
advantage of being quick and easy to prepare.

SERVES 4

3 tbsps oil
1 clove garlic, crushed
450g/1lb chicken meat, skinned, boned
   and diced
1 small red chilli pepper, seeded and diced
2 green peppers, diced
2 tbsps white wine
2 tbsps soy sauce
4 tbsps chicken stock
Pinch sugar (optional)
Salt
½ small can bamboo shoots, diced
1 tsp cornflour mixed with 3 tbsps water

1. Heat the oil in a large frying pan until
hot. Add the garlic and fry for 2-3 minutes.

2. Add the diced chicken, chilli, and
pepper, and stir well to coat with oil. Fry
for 6-7 minutes, when the chicken should
be almost cooked.

3. Add the white wine, soy sauce, chicken
stock, sugar and salt to the pan. Stir well
and add the bamboo shoots.

4. Cook for a further 2 minutes, add
cornflour and water and heat another
minute, stirring until the sauce has
thickened.

TIME: Preparation takes about 15 minutes, and cooking takes about 15 minutes.

SERVING IDEA: Accompany the dish with plain boiled rice, fried rice or Chinese noodles.

CHICKEN JUBILEE

*The sauce in this recipe is actually a
creative variation of a cherry dessert.*

SERVES 6

6 chicken breasts, skinned and boned
Oil
1 sprig fresh rosemary
Grated rind and juice of half a lemon
280ml/½ pint dry red wine
Salt and pepper
450g/1lb tinned or fresh black cherries,
    pitted
2 tsps cornflour
90ml/6 tbsps brandy

1. Heat about 60ml/4 tbsps oil in a sauté pan over moderate heat. Add the chicken breasts, skinned side down first. Cook until just lightly browned. Turn over and cook the second side for about 2 minutes.

2. Remove any oil remaining in the pan and add the rosemary, lemon rind, wine and salt and pepper. Bring to the boil and then lower the heat.

3. Add the cherries, draining well if tinned. Cook, covered, 15 minutes or until the chicken is tender. Remove the chicken and cherries and keep them warm. Discard the rosemary.

4. Mix the cornflour, lemon juice and some of the liquid from the cherries, if tinned. Add several spoonfuls of the hot sauce to the cornflour mixture. Return the mixture to the sauté pan and bring to the boil, stirring constantly, until thickened and cleared.

5. Pour the brandy into a metal ladle or a small saucepan. Heat quickly and ignite with a match. Pour over the chicken and cherries, shaking the pan gently until the flames subside. Serve immediately.

TIME: Preparation takes about 20 minutes if using pre-skinned and boned chicken breasts. Allow an extra 15 minutes to bone the chicken yourself.

PREPARATION: Serve the chicken dish on the day that it is cooked as it does not keep well. Add the brandy just before serving.

WATCHPOINT: When flaming spirits, always keep a pan lid handy in case the mixture flares up. In this case, quickly cover the pan and the flames will be smothered.

Index